# *Eaters of Flesh & Drinkers of Blood*

by Dr. Marlene Miles

Freshwater Press 2024

freshwaterpress9@gmail.com

ISBN: 978-1-965772-56-0

Paperback Version

# Table of Contents

# Eaters of Flesh & Drinkers of Blood

Freshwater

Freshwater Press, USA

# Introduction

This book was never intended to be fantastical or horrific. I warn you now if gory or gruesome things trigger you, do not read this book.

However, from the title and subject matter things certainly had to get gory and because of what needs to be addressed, things would definitely get messy.

We thank our Lord and Savior, Jesus Christ for redemption, for bringing us back from a sentence of death, hell, and the grave, and as we walk this life, we work out our salvation with fear and trembling, even against *eaters of flesh and drinkers of blood.*

# From Deuteronomy 7

Wherefore it shall come to pass, if ye hearken to these judgments, and keep, and do them, that the LORD thy God shall keep unto thee the covenant and the mercy which he sware unto thy fathers: And he will love thee, and bless thee, and multiply thee: he will also bless the fruit of thy womb, and the fruit of thy land, thy corn, and thy wine, and thine oil, the increase of thy kine, and the flocks of thy sheep, in the land which he sware unto thy fathers to give thee. Thou shalt be blessed above all people: there shall not be male or female barren among you, or among your cattle. And the LORD will take away from thee all sickness, and will put none of the evil diseases of Egypt, which thou knowest, upon thee; but will lay them upon all *them* that hate thee. And thou shalt consume all the people which the LORD thy God shall deliver thee; thine eye shall have no pity upon them: neither shalt thou serve their gods; for that *will be* a snare unto thee. If thou shalt say in thine heart, These nations *are* more than I; how can I dispossess them? Thou shalt not be afraid of them: *but* shalt well remember what the LORD thy God did unto Pharaoh, and unto all Egypt; (Deuteronomy 7:12-15)

Man is not supposed to be sick-- , like ever. But if he does get sick the Lord can heal all diseases.

Who forgiveth all thine iniquities; who healeth all thy diseases; (Psalm 103:3)

Life is in the blood. Your blood is supposed to be **in** your body, not on the outside of it, not anywhere else. Near it is not where it should be either. Life is in the blood; the blood should be **in** the body. This could be why so many people freak out when they see blood, it's supposed to be on the inside.

This book was spawned because of the numbers of teeth that I see lost. Will we have to give account for lost teeth? Will the Lord ask, *What happened here? What happened with the stewardship of your body?* Gall bladders, tonsils, spleens, appendices, and etcetera, as well as wisdom teeth and other teeth are lost every day. Will we have to give account for how we took care of our own physical body? If we have to give account for how we behaved spiritually, then how we took care of all that the Lord entrusted to us will be assessed. He gave us lordship over all the works of His hands.

We are the works of God's hands.

Yes, there are plenty of hospitals and there are surgeons who well know what they are doing to help people with these surgeries, but who is *sponsoring* them, who or what is causing the need for surgeries? Sickness and disease are a part of the Curse of the Law; they come with sin and its iniquity. We will have to answer for sin as well as the sequela of sin and its' iniquity.

Man is ever treating symptoms of things. Even if he thinks he has treated the root problem of a thing, he has most often treated the natural root of the problem and may have missed the spiritual root, if he is not a spiritual man. If you are suffering from a loathsome disease, what are the origins of that disease? Who or what would want any part of your body to be sick, ill, diseased, dysfunctional, bleeding, dying or even removed?

*There is* no
soundness in my flesh because of thine
anger; neither *is there*
*any* rest in my bones because of my sin.
(Psalm 38:3)

Man is not designed to carry disease. Disease belongs to the devil. Saved folks, God said He would not put disease on us. So where are they coming from? Sin. Iniquity. Heredity. The dark kingdom gets "permission" to bring diseases to those in sin, in those who carry iniquity. Once placed in a man's bloodline, it is in his foundation. This is how diseases are *inherited.*

For my loins are filled with a
loathsome *disease*: and *there is* no
soundness in my flesh. (Psalm 38:7)

1. My blood, be transfused with the Blood of Jesus, and reject every disease, in the Name of Jesus.
2. My foundation, be purged with the Blood of Jesus and reject every disease, in the Name of Jesus.
3. Any demon with access to the blood in, or any tissue of my body, or control over

it, your time is up, die, in the Name of Jesus.

4. Any demon with control over my monthly cycle, your time is up, fall down and die, in the Name of Jesus.

5. Any demon having impact in my life involving my physical body or flesh, hands off me, fall down and die, in the Name of Jesus.

6. Lord, heal my diseases, disorders, infirmities, sicknesses, and syndromes, in the Name of Jesus.

7. By the stripes of Jesus, I am healed, in the Name of Jesus.

# Eaters of Flesh and Drinkers of Blood

Who or what in the spirit world is looking for human blood or human flesh?

Evil entities.

Folks, the devil is either a mad scientist or he has mad scientists working for him to manipulate human blood and flesh to create new ways to destroy mankind, trick mankind, or, as it is said, to clone his own army for the end times because he hates women, and has no use for them.

Human blood and flesh are also used in evil rituals by witches, occultists, satanists, Luciferians and other evil human agents.

*Why does it matter, if it is in the spirit world?*

It matters because what happens in the spirit world if not dealt with will come into the natural world and cause mayhem, destruction, losses, and death, either to individuals or groups of people. It could affect entire nations, if not stopped. Most of the time, humans, without faith, wait until they can **see** it, then they want to create an answer for it. Watchmen, intercessors, prophets, prayer warriors, and deliverance ministers can see things while they are still in the spirit and pray to stop the evil and effect Godly changes for people and even nations.

If it does come to the natural by negligence of the person who was given signs or told about it, deliverance can still be possible, although some loss and or devastation may have already occurred. Still, we know God is our Healer, and He also can restore us, but so much depends on us, and on when it is seen, and addressed. It may take some time, but with God all things are possible.

These *spirits* called *eaters of flesh and drinkers of blood* either cause or allow evil men (and women) to do exactly what they do in the spirit, in the natural. In the natural, when we see or hear of a cannibal, know that an eater of flesh and a drinker of blood *spirit* is sponsoring them--, giving them a demonic idea or instruction and evil empowerment to carry out the act. Demons want blood, it is their "sacrifice." Those who have made deals with the devil are required to give or provide sacrifices to continue in the "relationship" they have started, and to keep from being killed themselves. When we see a literal headhunter, not someone in human resources recruiting others for jobs, but someone who hunts the heads of human beings, the *eaters of flesh and drinkers of blood* are behind it.

Sadly, ironic though that those who work in human resources are called headhunters. *Eaters of flesh and drinkers of blood* consume and want to consume the human virtues and resources of persons as they come to steal, kill, and destroy and viciously so. The ultimate and end game is to consume the actual, physical person.

What is an eater of flesh and a drinker of blood, anyway? They are evil *spirits* who come to do just what their names are called. They cause incidents and accidents, traumas, cuts, scrapes, homicide, suicides, and deaths, anything that draws blood or exposure or loss of blood, flesh, and life. Are you accident-prone? That could be these *spirits* trying to make you "accidentally" spill your own blood, or worse.

Flesh-eating bacteria and other diseases is the evil work of these evil *spirits* through the agents who work for them. Plagues, epidemics, pandemics, who is behind it? Whomever wants sickness and death, uses and feasts on either or both. They sponsor, or promote, or even with mad scientists in hell or the dark kingdom create these plagues. Because they are invisible, they don't seem to be attached to them; they are inherently occult, that is hidden. But something is behind all the blood loss and deaths of this world, and it is *eaters of flesh and drinkers of blood.*

The medical world whose living scientists are so proud of their brains, and they should be, will say it's the bacteria, viruses, fungi, etcetera, that overgrew, mutated or *whatever* and then caused *whatever* dread disease. Well, where did these bacteria or the rogue versions of these bacteria, come from? Why and how was it formed? And how did some unlucky person or some unlucky people roll up on it? For Christians, God says that He will NOT put diseases on us, so why are there so many diseases on so many people, *even Christians?* This includes heinous, mysterious, terminal, painful, and dread diseases.

God is not the author of that, the devil is. *Eaters of flesh and drinkers of blood* are the devil's agents in the spirit realm.

But surely, they don't come on like gangbusters. If you're to be their victim, they are more subtle; they don't want you to know that they are there, but if you ignore the signs and do nothing, soon they will be feasting at your painful expense.

If you are to be their evil human agent, the courtship is different, most of the time they'd rather you think that these perverse eating habits are your own idea whether formed in a drunken stupor, a drug induced frenzy, or through psychotic splits and schizophrenia that took years, decades or **lifetimes** to create. The sins of the father, unchecked, undealt with because of iniquity will be handed to the child of a bloodline and they will walk out the punishments and sequela of those sins, transgressions, and iniquities. It may take up to three or more generations to manipulate a bloodline into heinous acts against other humans by demons who were let in by the sins of the forefathers, and never dealt with.

Men who want to do perverse things with women on their periods, want the blood. If they say it's their *favorite time*, that is a serious warning, because God said to not do that at that time. Men who drink or otherwise acquire blood may have been promised **money, wealth, fame, power, or anything else** for doing this. It is a money ritual. There are all kinds, of money rituals, but blood-getting in any way, even by sex often is ritual. All illegal sex is ritual sex.

There are folks who have been initiated and believe they are vampires, or werewolves or other mythological beasts. Minds have been manipulated, stolen, or completely taken over so people do stone cold crazy things.

One gory example of cannibalism took place against the Serbs in concentration and death camps in Croatia(NDH), a Nazi puppet state governed by Ustashas who slit throats and drank the victims' blood. Whomever masterminded or directed this atrocity in the natural didn't just wake up one day and think of that; he may be the third, or so in his generation with ideas given to him by *eaters of flesh and drinkers of blood*, although that man who did it or directed it will take the blame in the natural. After all, his ancestors may already be deceased, and how do you prove this anyway?

The only way is by the Holy Spirit.

You already see that you need to pray about this whether anything medically tragic or inhumanely grotesque has happened in your family or not.

# Hansel & Gretel

As an adult, when you watch the cartoons you used to watch when you were a kid, you realize that there is a whole lot to those cartoons that you never saw, never realized, and never understood. Cartoons like **Bugs Bunny** had to have been made for adults, even though they were marketed as being for kids. That was then, but there is no shortage of animated films and stories that are made for adults and marketed as being for adults nowadays.

As you revisit the fairytales you read as a kid, you will see many things in them that you may not have seen as a child. I've always said that those fairytales aren't fairytales at all, but are true and packaged as children's stories, but tell deep and dark secrets that maybe could not have been told any other way.

Let's go back and visit the fairytale of Hansel and Gretel. The siblings, Hansel and Gretel, who are abandoned in a forest and fall into the hands of a witch who lives in a gingerbread, cake, and candy house. The evil witch plans to fatten the children before eating them.

Immediately there are several spiritual clues that must be looked at. Hansel and Gretel are in a forest. Being in a forest, lost in a forest, wandering in a forest, can't find one's way out of a forest, in a dream means that soul is captive. Does it not also mean that in the spirit, since in the dream one is in the spirit--, one is also captive?

Hansel and Gretel are siblings--, same mother and or father, which speaks of collective captivity. Were they destined by their foundation and their bloodline to become captives?

Hansel and Gretel are abandoned, by their parents, no less, and apparently they have no way out of this forest-witch dilemma.

This witch lives in a gingerbread and candy house, what could be more attractive to a couple of kids? Cookies, sweets, and candies. Was this witch a real person, or a spiritual entity? How does a real human live in a candy house, that has an oven, no less?

So, this witch is planning to fatten them up before eating them. There is nothing untrue about that. Even farmers fatten up animals before taking them to market or slaughtering them themselves. But, the witch is planning to eat these two children.

Hansel and Gretel may have been desperate, but they trusted a stranger and that stranger was a witch. But kids are not only trusting, but they are also taught to respect elders, some who should not be trusted. They are also at the mercy of big people who own all the houses, all the clothes, and all the food that they need for their own existence and survival. They also own all the candy, cakes, and all the gingerbread houses.

The story is also about parents who neglect and abandon their children, as well as those who will sacrifice children for their own selfish purposes and reasons.

Captives must do what their captors command them to do. I saw a video recently of African captives in the 1600s, who were brought to an island off the coast of Senegal and held there for three months before being shipped out to be sold into slavery in the Americas. How they happened to become captives is multi-storied, some were captured and sold by warring tribes who conquered them. Others were captured by the slave traders and taken to this stronghold where they were fattened up for sale. If they didn't fatten up to at least 130 pounds (the males) they couldn't bear the Middle Passage and be sold in the Western Hemisphere.

Hansel and Gretel were being fattened up for consumption. That old witch was an eater of flesh, although that is not stated in the fairytale.

The witch is the same as the devil whom the witch actually works for. The devil comes not but to steal, kill and destroy so people are fattened up for the kill. Fattened up to be stolen from, killed, destroyed. Even those who make devil deals will get a certain amount of success for some time period, but then they will be taken down. We see it all the time.

Gretel was not planning to be taken down by this witch, however. If you think about it, if their parents abandoned them and they were not only still alive, they were living it up in a cookie and candy house, eating all they wanted, they were a couple of shrewd kids who, so far, had outwitted fate.

So, Gretel outsmarts the witch more than once. First, when they are asked to put out their fingers, they use a twig or a bone that they've found on the property, so the witch still thinks they are skinny, doesn't kill them yet, and keeps feeding them. Witches are called blind witches if they don't know they are a witch. However, witches are known to be blind for a number of reasons. But we can deduce that sin makes anyone spiritually blind, and this may speak of the spiritual blindness of anyone involved in witchcraft. The devil and demons are not their friends and can never be. So, why can't they see that?

One day the witch is stoking the fire in the oven to roast Hansel. Gretel knows that the witch will cook her if she gets in the oven, so she pretends not to know how to do that. The witch sticks her own head into the oven to show Gretel, how it's done. That is Gretel's next trick, at that time, Gretel shoves her inside and latches the door. The witch burns to death, and Gretel rescues Hansel.

Suffer not a witch to live. (Exodus 22:18)

How they got back home after the escape when they had been abandoned by their parents is still a mystery to me. *Where's home? Do their parents even want them? Have their parents been looking for them?*

The book or story, **Hansel and Gretel** was challenged in California in 1992 because it teaches children that it is acceptable to kill witches, even though technically, in this story, it was self-defense because the witch was going to kill them. Those protesting the "fairytale" said it painted witches as child--eating monsters. Knowing what witches can do with demonic power, why should the book have been banned? Why did they have no concern for the **children**?

# Famine

There was a great famine in the 1300s during which people abandoned children. During the course of that famine, cannibalism may have been the fate of many. So, some of this story may have been rooted in truth, although it wasn't written until 1812 by the Brothers Grimm, and grim they were.

I will make mention in a few chapters from now of a woman who said she married a vampire. We can take that metaphorically as too many get into relationships or stay in relationships that are draining them. There are givers, that they call empaths, and then there are the takers, the narcissists. Those who are in relationships where the other person brings little or nothing to the table, and I'm not talking about money, the takers are especially draining. Those who offer no emotional support because they are emotionally distant or cold, or emotionally crippled will not add to your life or to the vitality of the relationship itself. The one will be constantly offering all the emotions, all the love, all the care while the other siphons off what they want and leaves the rest.

There are many kinds of famines, famines of attention, of love, relationship, companionship, joy. If one in a couple has none of that, the mistake a lot of people make is trying to bring all of that to the marriage, in hopes that the other person will "learn" how to be in a relationship.

Love is not merely learned; it is given, by God. If a person doesn't have a heart of flesh and a natural love for others, he needs God.

A woman spent more than a year creating a most stunning, thoughtful and really amazing gift for her special someone for a special occasion. Once it was presented to him, he glanced at it and threw it to the side. She knew this person very well, and knew his love language, so this gift should have hit the mark. Instead, he was not warm or compassionate enough to even receive the gift that was actually all about him. He had already siphoned what he wanted from that relationship and was really on his way out while she was still working hard to please him and show him what a loving relationship is all about. There was love famine in that "relationship," and the woman was abandoned emotionally—, left in the forest for whomever or whatever might *consume* her. He didn't care--, didn't give it a thought.

Aside from not being supported emotionally, not being appreciated, not having a *voice* in a relationship, every slam like that is a slap in the face, whether it is a slap in the face or not. The line from **The Color Purple** comes up again, *"You told Harpo to beat me?"* Yeah, it's the same as Harpo beating you. If you are not for me, you are against me, at least that is how it feels to the giver, who is usually soft-hearted.

In a relationship like that where one gives and gives and the other takes and takes, even when the giving is rejected, it still feels that one is being consumed while the other is enjoying life at the giver's full expense.

A bit of advice: aloof men (or women) may be intriguing and challenging, but they are not good choices for warm, long-term relationships.

# Vampires

The consummate *drinkers of blood* are vampires.

The world has worked tirelessly to make us believe that vampires and bloodthirsty creatures don't exist. So, where did vampires come from? Where did these stories come from? Vampires evolved from ghosts with bloodlust, to undead creatures with fangs and powers. Bram Stoker's Dracula is most responsible for our modern concepts of vampires.

Vampires are not called by name in the Bible. Neither are werewolves, zombies, and other such dangerous blood drinking or flesh-eating creatures. There are flesh tearing creatures in the Bible, and some of those devour flesh or are assigned to do so. But vampires and the like were prevalent in medieval folklore and ancient mythology, and seem to be universal, even in cultures that have never met or mixed.

Just as kids from all over the world feel that monsters are in the closet, or under their bed. Why is that? What are these kids seeing at night or in their dreams? Are they simply all watching the same TV shows? Well, some of these kids don't have TV's or even electricity for that matter. So???

Vampires are blood sucking corpses who reanimate somehow from their graves at night to drink the blood of humans. The more charismatic vampires that we see on the movie screen have consorts and they meet up or date, or whatever they do. The others attack sleeping humans, allegedly.

Hollywood has celebrated and romanticized vampires for decades and many have bought into it.

Mary Fairchild purports that one rather imaginative theory claims that vampires originated from two verses in the

Book of Genesis. It is not an erudite theory, and is far-fetched to me, but here it goes:

The legend of Lilith (Apocrypha) comes from a theory that Genesis has two creation accounts (Genesis 1:27 and 2:7, 20–22). Lilith is not mentioned by name in the Bible, but is only compared to a screech owl in Isaiah 34:14, as the first created woman, who refused to submit to Adam and fled from the Garden.

Eve was then created to be Adam's helper. After their expulsion from the garden, Adam reunited for a time with Lilith before finally returning to Eve. Lilith bore Adam a number of children, who became the *demons* of the Bible. According to kabbalistic legend, after Adam's reconciliation with Eve, Lilith took the title Queen of the Demons and became a murderer of infants and young boys, whom she turned into vampires.

By now you may be wondering, *Is it okay for a Christian to read vampire books? I mean, vampires are not in the Bible, and its only fiction, right?*

My answer is: If you find a "Christian vampire," let me know. I'm grieved enough just researching this book, I wouldn't seek this stuff out for entertainment.

It is up to **you** to guard the gates of your life--, your ear gates, your eye gates. It is up to you to guard your mind. It is up to you to think only on those things that have virtue and a good report. Many teenagers and young adults have been pulled into the vampire stories and may have fascination with or be obsessed, further leading them into the *occult*. Adding romance to occultic things, such as vampires, adds power to these creatures, and makes them a *gateway* fantasy.

**This is so not cool.**

Vampirism is occultic, along with witchcraft, astrology, spiritualism, Tarot card readings, palmistry, numerology, voodoo, mysticism, and et cetera.

And now, dear brothers and sisters, one final thing. Fix your thoughts on what is true, and honorable, and right, and pure, and lovely, and admirable. Think about things that are excellent and worthy of praise. (Philippians 4:8 NLT)

Romanticizing vampires and werewolves, which we will discuss later, normalizes, and elevates these creatures to a human status and even to idolatry as they are often the leading characters in vampire and werewolf books and movies. It also desensitizes humans to the dangers and occult powers that these beings have.

Beings from the dark kingdom do not have love; Love is a gift of God. They don't love and can't love, and they especially can't love mankind; they hate mankind. . Why would there be a heartthrob leading man in a movie if he has no heart? If he can't love, what is the purpose of this?

However, leading characters in movies are usually charming, handsome, buff, good-looking, rich, and many times sexy, which appeals to the fantasies of many--, too many. All this makes the idolater gloss over the fact that these are demons who wield dark powers in the dark shadows and are very dangerous to life, purpose, and destiny of real humans. As well they are totally opposed to the plan of God.

It's like being hypnotized; everything is cleverly framed, cleverly presented, but it hypnotizes the reader or watcher who lets down their guards, ceasing to guard their Gates and lets this dashing or pitiful "character," depending on how it is portrayed, into the world of their mind and soul.

*What have they let in?*

In the case of vampires, or the *idea* of vampires, they've let in *drinkers of blood.* In the case of the *vampiric spirit--,* the same thing, *drinkers of blood.* All because of a romp or two into darkness. Those of the light should have no communion with the darkness, just as Diana in Genesis went out, alone, one day to see the daughters of the land. Diana went out to frolic among some idols. She never should have had any communion with idols.

"I am the light of the world. If you follow me, you won't have to walk in darkness, because you will have the light that leads to life." (John 8:12, NLT)

Idols and demons are not always ferocious and demanding at the beginning.

They know how to romance humans and draw them in. Not only that, humans, when doing all of this cavorting or frolicking with the dark side are totally on their own, like Diana; they are in their flesh because if you were not *sent by God*, then you went of your own volition and you are on your own. Idols, devils, demons and such like have power. They have real power,—both the power to attract and charm, but if that doesn't work, they change up and use that power to steal, kill, and destroy. If you like the romantic, charming side of their power, know that it won't last. Even in a human-to-human relationship the honeymoon phase is wonderful, but then reality must set in.

Humans and demons are not made to mate, date, or have romantic encounters or relationships. There is no real honeymoon— it is all an act, and you should not be doing anything with any of them, even in your mind. A vampire cannot be a heartthrob. You cannot have a crush on a werewolf, these are dangerous beings. If you don't believe they are beings, then they are dangerous *spirits* that you should have no communion with.

Walk in the light while you can, so the darkness will not overtake you. Those who walk in the darkness cannot see where they are going. (John 12:35 NLT)

Parents are wise to prayerfully consider the risks of allowing a child unsupervised exposure to vampire fiction. You need to know how to speak to your child because if you tell him that he definitely can't watch it, he may do just the opposite of what you said, just because you said it and he is now tempted.

Teach your child at all times. *Because I said* so is not a good enough reason for a child to not do something. So, teach your child why you say yes or no to a thing, especially when you say, *No.*

# She Married a Vampire

One such person who said she became infatuated with vampires at an early age is a woman named Patrice Bates. She gives a powerful video testimony on You Tube about how she married a vampire.(See it for yourself: https://www.youtube.com/watch?v=qvakwG8lEaA )

I won't lie, I watched **Dark Shadows** growing up and I was petrified the whole time but kept watching it. One night they had a marathon where Barnabus Collins and Angelique *vampired* it up from dusk to the next dawn. As a high schooler, I stayed up by myself all night and watched it. The only good that came out of it was that I never wanted to watch another horror show or movie ever again. I mean, **ever**.

Being a teenager and not knowing anything about romance, really, we may

think that biting on the neck is kinda hot –
didn't we get hickeys back then that we tried
to hide from our parents? This wasn't really
sex, but it was closeness with the opposite
gender, so it was very intriguing without
literally looking like a sin. And it was made
to be that way; demonically so. But we may
have been too young and too stupid to realize
what we may have been getting initiated into.
While we may have been thinking all of this,
we were also thinking that this is fake, it's not
real, and so what, it's only make-believe.

But it was so much more than that.
This creature is killing the person, not all at
once, but sucking the life out of them. The
vampire movie is a snuff film, by degrees and
in slow motion. Why should we watch that?

Lord, forbid.

The woman who gave a testimony
that she married a vampire seemed very
truthful and had a way with words. She said
that that husband was draining her, and then
described how he did that.

A person with a *vampiric spirit* wants
your life. They want your lifeforce. It may

start out as a dismantling of sorts; they want to see how you work, what makes you tick, so they can take you apart and make sure you don't tick anymore. Do they realize that they are doing it? Maybe. Some may, others may not, but they are still doing it.

They are taking another's blood while still keeping their own; it's not a transfusion, it is the taking of blood which should no more be allowed than the taking of one's breath. Just as breath makes one alive; the life is in the Blood. Oxygen, which is the reason we breathe, is in the blood, so now you see how life is in the blood?

# Bleeding Disorders

If a *bloodsucker* can't get to your neck, or get you comfortable enough to let them get to your neck, he may have to devise other ways to get your blood. The devil is very tricky, so don't think he hasn't evolved in his devilments to get blood and drain the lifeforce out of people.

If the devil can't get to your blood, perhaps he'll try to get your blood to come to him. *How so?* Involuntary bleeding--, when a person bleeds involuntarily how does that happen? Is that something to be concerned about?

*Yes, of course.*

A bleeding disorder in the natural could be the reason why a person bleeds sporadically, easily, or seemingly spontaneously, and or doesn't clot properly if they do bleed.

Bleeding disorders affect clotting times, which slows down the way the blood clots which is called coagulation. Certain diseases and conditions prevent blood from clotting properly, which can result in heavy or prolonged bleeding.

In the natural, clotting disorders can cause abnormal bleeding visibly, that is on the outside of the body, and internally, inside the body. Bruising is the aggregation of blood beneath the skin. So is petechia, purpura, contusions, hematoma--, there are so many types of this. The devil is busy.

For proper clotting, the body needs clotting factors, along with platelets which are normally in the blood cells. Platelets clump together to form a plug at the site of the injury or the bleeding. For example, a blood clot forms after a tooth is extracted to make the bleeding stop and make the healing begin. The fibrin clot seals the blood vessels or capillaries that may be bleeding.

Those with bleeding disorders don't clot correctly and will continue to bleed. This will delay healing and is the cause of a dry socket as in a dental extraction. It is also very painful as the protective clot is lost.

Loss of a blood clot can be by error of the patient as well. If the instructions for aftercare are not followed the clot can be dislodged and the vessels at the extraction site will again be exposed and bleeding may start up again. The bleeding doesn't always resume, but without the fibrin clot, the raw extraction site is now exposed.

Improper clotting, or loss of a blood clot can also lead to bleeding into the muscles, joints, or other parts of the body.

Most bleeding disorders are inherited, passed from parent to child. Saints, whatever is in your blood that is inherited is also spiritual, else it wouldn't be in there.

Diseases that lead to bleeding can be caused by a low red blood cell count, potassium deficiency, or liver disease. Certain medications may lead to bleeding or excessive bleeding.

Hemophilia is a reason for excessive bleeding that can leak into the joints. Von Willebrand's disease is the most commonly inherited bleeding disorder. People with that disorder have blood that lacks what is needed to clot.

Signs of being afflicted with a bleeding disorder show up as multiple bruises, bruising easily, heavy menstrual periods, frequent nosebleeds that may or may not be due to high blood pressure. A person with a bleeding disorder could have excessive bleeding from even small lesions.

In these ways a person can bleed involuntarily, or bleed more or longer than they should. And, these are some of the ways that blood is either made available for *drinkers of blood*, or in the spirit if *drinkers of blood* are at work, these are signs in the natural that **the person is under attack by thee** *spirits*.

Yes, I am saying that if you are bleeding excessively or more often than you should, especially if you are a woman, suspect that *drinkers of blood* and their cohorts, eaters of flesh are at work in your life and body. They won't just eat flesh and drink blood; they eat up every good thing that is assigned to your life. They suck up and eat up every blessing from God that should be yours. When you get something good, it is lost because of *eaters of flesh and drinkers of blood.*

Look very closely at your body. Are you losing things and you feel or know it is unnatural for you to lose them? Teeth? Hair? Are your organs working properly or is something under threat of malfunctioning or being lost? Are you indeed exhausted and feeling drained?

Haven't you heard people say they were hemorrhaging money, for example? Where do you think their money is going, or how do you think it is going? No one actually bleeds money.

They are being ripped off by *drinkers of blood* in the spiritual realm and then it is manifesting in the natural realm.

Suspect *eaters of flesh and drinkers of blood.*

# Trauma

If the men of my tabernacle said not, Oh that we had of his flesh! we cannot be satisfied (Job 31:31)

Trauma is always a devil move. It's done for soulish reasons; the devil likes to stun and astonish people with sudden terror and sudden destruction. This opens up their spirits and souls so he can get in or send in some other demon or demons. But trauma is also used by the devil for physical reasons. Many kinds of trauma can cause bleeding in a person, obviously. Trauma can also cause internal, unseen bleeding; this is very attractive to these *eaters of flesh and drinkers of blood.*

Other trauma to the physical body may be inflicted by evil agents or they could be self-inflicted, unfortunately. Boils, pimples, skin lesions, hemorrhoids, cuts, scrapes, abrasions--, anything that bleeds is a magnet for eaters of flesh and *drinkers of blood*.

They will run to the blood. Like moths to a flame, like wild birds to seed, eaters of flesh and *drinkers of blood*, like vultures, will run or fly to blood.

And Elijah said unto the prophets of Baal, Choose you one bullock for yourselves, and dress *it* first; for ye *are* many; and call on the name of your gods, but put no fire *under*. And they took the bullock which was given them, and they dressed *it*, and called on the name of Baal from morning even until noon, saying, O Baal, hear us. But *there was* no voice, nor any that answered. And they leaped upon the altar which was made. And it came to pass at noon, that Elijah mocked them, and said, Cry aloud: for he *is* a god; either he is talking, or he is pursuing, or he is in a journey, *or* peradventure he sleepeth, and must be awaked. **And they cried aloud, and cut themselves after their manner with knives and lancets, till the blood gushed out upon them.** And it came to pass, when midday was past, and they prophesied until the *time* of the offering of the *evening* sacrifice, that *there* *was* neither voice, nor any to answer, nor any that regarded. (1 Kings 18:25-29)

The evil prophets of Baal cut themselves to draw blood because the blood would draw *spirits* that they thought they could invoke to do their evil bidding. Cutting oneself is demonic; a person who does this needs deliverance and not just a counselor or a psychologist to talk to.

A grown man in his 40's with eczema would scratch and scratch until he bled; he did this daily. Once the bleeding started and got under his fingernails, he would put his bloody finger in his mouth and suck the blood off of it. Gross! How many years had he been doing this?

Spiritually, do you wonder who was sponsoring that bizarre behavior?

# Diagnosis

If you have a bleeding disorder you may seek medical care. After taking a complete medical history, the doctor will run several tests. CBC, a complete blood count, PAT, platelet aggregation test, and bleeding time test.

If this is completely spiritual, the patient will get a clean bill of health, and it will be told to him or her that there is nothing wrong with them. All their tests will be normal. In that case, this is not a physical, medical, or physiological problem, it is spiritual and should be handled that way. But let's say the patient is told they have a bleeding disorder---.

Treatment options vary depending on the type of bleeding disorder and its severity.

Though treatments can't cure bleeding disorders, they can help relieve the symptoms.

**<u>God</u> can cure bleeding disorders**, because they are spiritual in origin--, really all diseases are spiritual in origin. The spiritual cause may not be anything you have done, but something you <u>inherited</u>. As well, there is a spiritual origin to blood finding its way OUT of your body instead of staying **in** your body. .

Iron supplements may be recommended for the anemic patient who is chronically anemic. This condition can make a person feel weak, tired, and dizzy. One of my favorite patients has ice cold hands. She usually grabs my hands when I greet her because she likes how warm my hands are. It takes us a few minutes to separate so I can begin to work on her. I happen to also know that she is praying for me and my hands before I work on her. She is a wise woman.

So, I asked her, "Has your PC doc checked your iron levels?"

She said, nobody has ever asked me that, so I'm going to ask him. On the next visit her hands were nearer to normal; they were cool, but not cold. She was now on iron supplements.

There are other treatment modalities for anemia, which we won't labor on since we are most interested in the ***spiritual*** causes and solutions to bleeding and or blood loss.

Complications can also arise if the disorder is severe or causes excessive blood loss. Bleeding disorders can be dangerous for all, but for women it increases the risk of excessive bleeding in childbirth, a miscarriage, or a spontaneous abortion. Women with bleeding disorders may also experience very heavy menstrual bleeding. This can lead to anemia which can cause general weakness, shortness of breath, and dizziness.

Women with bleeding disorders often have one or more of these signs or symptoms.

Heavy bleeding during menstruation (period) lasting more than 7 days. Passing blood clots in the cycle that are bigger than a grape. Soaking a tampon or a pad every hour or more often on the heaviest day(s).

- Nosebleeds for no apparent reason, lasting longer than 10 minutes, or that need medical attention.

- Easily bruised, even with no physical injury.

- Waking up in the morning with new bruises, cuts, or scratches that you didn't go to bed with and there is no human in the bed with you.

- Excessive bleeding after a medical procedure or dental extraction; and

- A history of muscle or joint bleeding with no physical injury.

Of all the things the doctor can do to help you treat the symptoms of bleeding disorders, these disorders are not cured. Don't you find that to be a curiosity? They can't be cured by medical personnel and medications because they are **spiritual**. The doctor doesn't do spiritual things, therefore we need to pray and invoke the power of God and the Help of our Helper, the Holy Spirit to heal and deliver us, after all He is the Spirit of Deliverance. Else, this may lead to the continuous loss of blood.

Spiritually, this is far more than the loss of blood, it is like putting out food for a stray cat. What you draw to yourself will be far worse than a wayward domesticated or feral animal. If there is bleeding, the *eaters of flesh and the drinkers of blood* will be feasting. If feasting, they are growing and increasing.

Lord, forbid.

# Occult Blood

Why do you think they call unknown or hidden blood *occult*? Why do doctors check for occult blood? It is because the blood is hidden and not obvious. When something is hidden, you have to diagnose by signs and symptoms and various tests. For thought: could it be called occult blood because that's who caused it or who is benefitting from it?—occultic agents?

*Occult* blood can be in the urine. It can be in the stool. It can be from any number of places within the body, such as a bleeding ulcer in the GI tract.

Too many things can bleed in the body and a person not really be aware of it. Internal bleeding symptoms include severe pain, dizziness, swelling, and coughing up blood, depending on the affected area and the rate of blood loss. You might suspect internal bleeding if you experience unexplained weakness, persistent pain, or signs like swelling and discoloration without an obvious injury.

I am telling you all of this so if you have these types of symptoms, you will know how to pray. When you suspect *eaters of flesh and drinkers of blood*, you don't just say you're falling apart. You will pray accordingly. There are prayers throughout this book and in the prayer section at the end.

Different types of trauma and fractures can cause undetected internal bleeding. Ruptured blood vessels (aneurysms) can be a culprit. Drugs such as blood thinners and anticoagulants can contribute to internal bleeding. Certain viruses may cause it.

If a woman has endometriosis, she may have heavy blood flow that she cannot even see because it is hidden in the abdominal or pelvic area. Other areas that might bleed are:

- bleeding in the intestines
- bleeding into the brain
- bleeding in the mouth, from the gums
- bleeding into the joints

You can't see blood when any of this is happening, but there is still bleeding. Bleeding is a marker for *eaters of flesh and drinkers of blood* because they are looking for blood. The freer it is flowing the more they like that situation and will be drawn to it.

The loss of blood as well as the presence of blood, even a little bit of it can draw the *eaters of flesh and the drinkers of blood.*

*Such as?*

Gingivitis, periodontal disease causes the presence of occult blood in the mouth of those infected with either of these diseases. The severity, the duration, and the level of disease affects if there is blood in the mouth, how much, when, and if you can see it or not. Many times, the person who has this disorder can taste it; it tastes metallic. Over time, the jawbone is diminished in the person who has gingivitis which leads to more severe periodontal disease. The bone of the jaw can be lost by millimeters which doesn't sound like much, but it is. After bone loss, the person loses teeth. They can be lost by infection, or just by loss of attachment--, they just get loose and fall out or have to be removed. *Eaters of flesh and drinkers of blood.*

Again, I ask if you think the Lord will ask us what happened to our Earth teeth when we get to Glory? Yes, we should be in a glorified body, but will we have to give account of being unaware of *eaters of flesh and drinkers of blood,* and or doing nothing about it? It's not that serious you may say. *Oh, it isn't?*

Bacteria and genetics are the culprits of gum diseases in the natural, but who would want access to human blood 24/7? Who is drawn to it? *Eaters of flesh and drinkers of blood.* Aside from dental care, and diligent home care, be sure to pray or get prayer against these demons.

There are many signs and symptoms which we won't cover in this book since this is not a medical course. Mostly we want to look at the **spiritual** cause for any of these things. Ask yourself, who would want these things to happen to anyone?

The Evil One.
*For what purpose?*

For the *eaters of flesh and drinkers of blood.*

The loss of blood can lead to severe medical complications, physical limitations, organ damage, organ failure, or worse. Spiritually it is a slow or gradual loss of vitality.

In the early stages of pregnancy, bleeding may be the sign of a miscarriage, or ectopic pregnancy, placenta previa, placental abruptions, or uterine rupture can cause internal bleeding. Oh, it's serious. *Eaters of flesh and drinkers of blood* interfere with a woman getting pregnant and staying pregnant for a healthy delivery. So, this is very serious. Like the witch in Hansel and Gretel and many others that we will read about, **they come for the children**, especially.

Complications like these often cause vaginal bleeding, but not always. Bleeding may be concealed behind the placenta, increasing the risk of a late diagnosis and death.

I had a patient call to cancel his dental appointment scheduled for that day because he said he had internal bleeding. Miraculously, he was fine the next day and came in for dental care. Some very mild cases of internal bleeding may resolve naturally if the body forms clots to stop the bleeding.

Christians, for best results, PRAY!

Please note, just because a thing is spiritual and you have faith, it doesn't mean that you do not seek medical diagnosis, advice, and treatment.

# Werewolves

8. Lord, let every devourer be devoured, in the Name of Jesus.

**If this book wasn't weird enough, I must bring out other things for your consideration.**

*Werewolf* literally means man-wolf. From ancient mythology we learn that Ishtar was rejected by a man who she then turned into a wolf. In ancient Rome anyone who was believed to have been turned into a wolf by means of magic spells or herbs was called *versipellis* which means *turnskin*. This is ironic because the two who are given credit for discovering Rome are Romulus and Remus who were raised by a wolf. *Go figure.*

Werewolves and other shape-shifters appear in folklore worldwide. **Werewolves**

**and other devouring and tearing beasts** tear and eat flesh. What do wolves especially like? Sheep. This is no coincidence, saints of God.

> Who also eat the flesh of my people, and
> flay their skin from off them; and they
> break their bones, and chop them in
> pieces, as for the pot, and
> as flesh within the caldron. (Micah 3:3)

They say werewolves are the things of folklore and nightmares. Yet, pretty much every culture has them. Cultures that don't know each other, don't mix, don't speak the same language and are not near one another all have werewolves in their folklore. There is a new movie out, as a comedy, in the USA about a woman who turns into a doglike creature at night. So, we see it either never stops or it is hard to stop this kind of movie or storytelling in even polite society.

Have people seen, and do people see these beasts in their dreams? And, if so, why? Who is showing this to folks? Are these demonic dreams of what the devil wants to do to people? Are they divine dreams of the Lord showing people that this is what is coming your way if you don't change, repent, seek the Lord, and pray?

It varies from person to person and from case to case.

In movies the storylines vary from focusing on the person who is cursed to change into this animal-like creature, or it focuses on the victim or victims who are of course petrified of the creature who has bitten or scratched them and initiating them into werewolf beastdom. (*Beastdom--*, is that a word?) Changing into a werewolf by this means has a name, *lycanthropy,* coined as early as the year 27 by Petronius and has continued to be used through the centuries and even today.

From Europe the folklore of werewolves spread by Colonialism. Well folks, just as there were witch hunts in Europe and the States, there were werewolf hunts. Persecution, if you want to call it that, seems to be equal opportunity for males and females. Many times, when spiritual things are not understood, people are blamed and persecuted. Many times, people are rightly accused, other times they are falsely accused.

There is the case of Peter Stumpp and many other males who were accused and convicted as well as killed by burning at the stake or hanging. These people were also accused of wolf-riding and wolf-charming. This guy, Stumpp, the Werewolf of Bedburg, was executed in 1589 for cannibalism and other crimes.

Werewolves are known to be avid hunters just by virtue of their bloodlust or blood thirst. They must hunt, at least that is how it is depicted by Hollywood. Folks are we not still talking about *eaters of flesh and drinkers of blood*? When people don't know what to call a thing, they will make up something. When people don't understand visions and dreams, they will create something that seems to solve the problem.

Werewolves are bad enough, but there are *Weretigers* in India. Germany was most obsessed with werewolves, and they believed that a person could turn into an animal for 7 years.

Can it not? That happened to King Nebuchadnezzar who was turned into a grazing beast for 7 years, in the Book of Daniel. If God can do a thing, or if God has done it, wouldn't the devil try to copy it?

Zeus turned someone into a wolf who tried to feed him human flesh. People, human flesh is what is fed to dreamers in the dream. The purpose of that is to indoctrinate or initiate a person into the coven, into witchcraft. Spit it out, vomit it up, pray fervently against evil spiritual food when or if that happens to you in the dream.

If you do what they do; if you eat flesh you should not eat, or eat food sacrificed to idols you are now one of them and you are, in essence, worshipping that idol.

Online, I saw a blog where a guy had come up with 10 reasons why people eat in the dream and none of them were spiritually accurate as it concerns deliverance. Never once did the writer suggest that the person needed deliverance. It was all surface and fluffy. That is the nature of worldly dream interpretation, nothing is really serious, nothing is immediate, or imminent. Nothing is disastrous… or anything to pray against. So don't believe worldly dream interpretation if you are having real spiritual troubles that need to be resolved.

The Hollywood movie **Wolverine** makes the main character into a hero. In the movies, a bite or a curse is the initiation. It turns a person into something that they don't want to be, and they are cursed to mostly attack people they know and are supposed to love.

According to the movie, **Wolfman,** the only way to stop a werewolf is a silver bullet to the heart, or with Fire, or beheading, which are the same ways that a vampire is killed.

**With God, we just pray, and seek deliverance because whatever the creature *appears* as, or if it appears at all, since it is really invisible, it is still an eater of flesh and a drinker of blood and must be dealt with.**

I say all of this because beasts and monsters can occur in dreams. Dreams can be repetitive. The devil is adept at sending dream masquerades to make things seem true that are not true about people that the dreamer actually knows. And etcetera.

In the meantime, the devil has put false images on a person's dream screensaver, while he may actually be doing the very thing that he is showing the dreamer. When the dreamer is awake, he is focusing on a lie, whether a lie about another person or various persons, while the devil is having his way with the one who dreams.

*How can this be?*

The dream is a horror, a nightmare. If the dreamer is not casting it down, the dreamer is getting faith for that sort of thing. Fear is a negative faith, but it is faith. Fear draws the thing the person fears. *Greatly fearing* greatly draws that thing. The devil is showing the person what he wants to do to him or to the village or community. If this person is a person of authority there, but doing nothing about it, he is negligent. The dreamer is chasing the wrong thing or things in his awake life, while the devil tears up the man or the town.

No! You may argue that whatever happens in the physical realm must come through a person, so fighting against these werewolves is necessary. Well, that's when it gets to the natural realm. Until it gets there, it is happening in the spirit, so if the spirit is not being addressed, it's still coming--, whether through the face in the dream, if it is a masquerade or via some other route. So the fighter has fought the hologram of the real thing, instead of fighting the hologram while it was a hologram in the spirit so it would never manifest itself in the natural.

That werewolf fighter might even stay up night after night out in the streets or the woods looking for or chasing these beasts. In this way he is not getting his spiritual updates on the state of werewolves in his life, you know, those beasts that tear and rip, and bite, and kill--, because he is not sleeping. Specifically, he is not getting REM sleep, so he may be missing every spiritual update. This is as good as the devil wants it.

An ounce of prevention is worth a pound of cure.

Strange attacks and gruesome killings led to medieval werewolf trials in the 15$^{th}$ to 18$^{th}$ centuries. If crops failed, livestock died, or people disappeared, werewolves were to blame. In France and Switzerland dozens of people were killed after being accused of being werewolves. Executions, burning at the stake, beheadings, just as in the witch trials.

In Spain, Manuel Blanca Romasanta a drifter confessed to killing 13 people in the mid 1800's. He said he turned into a werewolf when he killed. Turning into a werewolf is called lycanthropy.

There was an alleged werewolf in the USA in the 1990's, in Wisconsin called the Beast of Brae Road.

In France, some gruesome murders were never solved. Also in France, in 1521, two Frenchmen were executed for murder and lycanthropy after they admitted having killed and eaten six children while transformed into werewolves.

The Werewolf of Dole, was executed in 1573 for strangling four children and eating their flesh. An unidentified man was burned at the stake in 1598 for the murders of 50 children in France after their remains were found in his home.

A French teenager claimed in 1603 that he was a werewolf, and that he had killed and eaten various children who had recently gone missing.

Sometime between the 1300s and the 1800s, in Germany, two children, Hansel and Gretel were to be killed and eaten by a woman who obviously was a witch, but they outwitted her and got away. If that is based on a real story, we would have had to add those two children, Hansel and Gretel, to the statistics of gruesome murders inspired by *eaters of flesh and drinkers of blood.*

# Shapeshifters

Shapeshifters exist. Anyone who has ever had a dream and seen this, know, if it is happening in the spirit, God is either showing you something or allowing you to see something that you <u>need</u> to see. The most remembered dream that my grandma told us was that she saw a man in her dream turn into a white dog, or a dog turn into a man. The details escape me right now, but it was the most amazing dream we had heard as kids.

That was shapeshifting. Werewolves, if they really exist, are shapeshifters.

Grandma's dream is useful information because it helps our family to do spiritual mapping our family. But another take away from it is that shapeshifting is a thing, and it happens, whether you've seen it to remember it or not.

Criminals and movie villains have often wanted shapeshifting abilities. Why? To do crimes of course and get away with them. Who would bestow such a power? Whoever has that power and has it up for barter or sale. Who would give it to an evil person? An evil power would, of course.

In the Bible we may call that transformation or transfiguration. Is it not shapeshifting? In Africa, but probably not just in Africa, they say certain ones can turn into hyenas or other animals. What do hyenas and most wild animals do? They hunt, they tear flesh, they eat it. They are *eaters of flesh* and surely, they lap the blood as well.

In a sense, a shapeshifter is a person who can look the same day after day, but their personality is different depending on who they are today and what they are going through, or what they plan to take you through.

Jesus is the same yesterday, today and forever. So, you know who is doing all this shapeshifting; it's the one who can appear as an angel of light—the devil and his crew.

# Roaming Lion

Be alert and of sober mind. Your enemy the
devil prowls around like a roaring
lion looking for someone to devour. (1 Peter
5:8)

The roaring lion has been roaming
about seeking whom he may destroy and
devourer. The Devourer in the Bible, what do
you think he is coming to devour?

Everything and anything, most likely.

9. Therefore, devourers you shall be
   devoured, people who want to devour
   you will be devoured, in the mighty name
   of Jesus. (Jeremiah 30:16)
10. Anyone who wants to devour me, let
    them be devoured, in the Name of Jesus.

In the wild, hyenas will even attack
lions to try to take the prey of the mighty lion

away. Shall the prey escape? Well not from a lion *and* a hyena—people please.

A vagrant was arrested in <u>Połomia</u> for murdering a 14-year-old girl and eating parts of her body. He also admitted to having killed and eaten five other people since 1846 that he had dug up from Parisian cemeteries.

At least 29 albino Tanzanians were murdered between 2007 and 2008 out of a "belief that potions made from albinos' legs, hair, hands, and blood can make a person rich. Do people doing spells and money rituals think things all the way through? If the albino thing were true, wouldn't all albinos already be rich just by virtue of owning those body parts?

A group of men cut off the legs of a young albino child before slitting its throat, and then drinking the blood.

Another man was arrested while transporting an albino baby's head to a witch doctor who had offered to pay for it.

The evil and madness of men must be checked. **Lord, help us all.**

# In the Cooker

But flesh with the life thereof, *which is* the blood thereof, shall ye not eat. (Genesis 9:4)

In the story of Hansel and Gretel, the witch was planning to cook Hansel and then eat him. So, do these *eaters of flesh* cook things first, or do they eat things raw? Since they are eating things spiritually and not in the natural, does it matter?

Have you noticed a part of your body running hot all the time? On deliverance grounds they say that means that that part of your body is in the cauldron, and it is being *cooked.* All of this sounds fantastical and also horrific, but I am reporting and recording it for your instruction and edification. If it doesn't apply to you, thank God. If it does, at least now you may have a point of reference and more understanding of what may be going on and how to pray about it. Either way, that "hot" part of your body, if it is not menopause may be telling you to pray because infection may be present in that body part. If it doesn't resolve after prayers, then seek medical attention. If nothing is found to be a medical problem, then continue to pray and seek deliverance.

Menopause? Hot flashes? Is this a lot of devil plantations coming home to roost. By the Holy Spirit I learned that a lot of senior and older "diseases" are from old spiritual food that was eaten in the dream over the life of a person but was never dealt with. (See my book **ESF: Getting Rid of Evil Spiritual Food.** Even after you get rid of evil spiritual food that was eaten in the dream, they could still come back with more and more. Think about it, *eaters of flesh and drinkers of blood*, like the witch in the fairytale of Hansel and Gretel will continue to fatten their intended prey, until you get rid of them permanently. Don't let that prey be you.

Shall the prey be taken from the mighty, or the lawful captive delivered? (Isaiah 49:24)

# Cannibalism

**11. Father, by the power of Your Spirit cover the minds, souls, bodies and spirits of all who enter to read this chapter and those before and after as this turns gruesome. While it was never the intent of this book, these are things we should know as not be remain ignorant. Purge our souls, bodies, and spirits of all things demonic and devilish that we are not initiated or indoctrinated into any dark practices or desires, in the Name of Jesus. Amen.**

Carnivores are humans that eat meat. Specifically, cannibals are humans that eat humans--, the ultimate *eater of flesh*. A cannibal is any who eats the flesh of its own specie. Having to eat another human is part of the Curse of the Law. Choosing to eat another human is demonic and it's because of a curse and brings on other curses. When curses are so layered that a person is nearly buried it may seem impossible, but as long as there is life, there is hope.

**Lord, help!**

The Bible warns as in the case of famine that people may have to eat their children or one another. God does not lie. The devil, of course, will take every wicked thing to extreme if he is allowed.

The king replied, "If the Lord does not help you, where can I get help for you? From the threshing floor? From the winepress?" Then he asked her, "What's the matter?"

She answered, "This woman said to me, 'Give up your son so we may eat him today, and tomorrow we'll eat my son.' So we cooked my son and ate him. The next day I said to her, 'Give up your son so we may eat him,' but she had hidden him."
(2 Kings 6:27-29)

People in Africa get accused of so many things. But, at the same time, Africa has been there and much of it without the

Lord God for so long that they have leaned to their own understanding and to the instruction of lesser, and evil *gods*. Because of that, they may have done so many atrocities that it has made those of us who think we are *civilized* very afraid.

Again, we run into Hollywood and other filmmakers who turn the idea of cannibalism into horror films. That is not my cup of tea, but folks, they are out there. As horrible as all this is in this book, why anyone would want to add lies and deception to it by watching fictional films is not understandable to this writer. Well, except that they are instructed by the devil to do so. One particular film was so bad that the director was charged with murder and accused of having made a snuff film. Unfortunately, snuff films exist too, for the blood and for the flesh, but also for the trauma which the devil uses every day for his own purposes. That is the subject of yet another book.

So remote African and other tribes are accused of cannibalism, have been for centuries. But it is not just Africans, no, not by a long shot.

- During the siege of Jerusalem in 70 CE, a woman named Mary of Bethezuba was said to have cannibalized her infant son due to starvation. So, cannibalism was done in Bible days.
- Brits did it.
- It was done in Rome during a siege in 409. "The starving people tore each other limb from limb that they might have flesh to eat. Even the mother did not spare the babe at her breast."
- The city's population shrank from 800,000 inhabitants before the sieges to less than half of that nine years later. Natural causes or demonic intervention?
- In the sixth century, China allowed prisoners of war to be traded for food. The Chinese did it. One later account is that "the rich competed in wealth, a sport that included competition over cannibalism" as one way of surprising one's guests with exotic novelty food.

My point is that this has always been done, so why should any of us, including myself be shocked? We should be doing something about it if possible, if not to at least protect ourselves and our loved ones.

- Hind attempted to eat the liver of Muhummad which the liver was considered to be the *seat of life*.
- The Irish did it during a severe famine in 698–700. And also documented in 1116.

## It was done in the Middle Ages

- The Danes did it when being starved out by William the Conqueror.
- Some crusaders did it during the sieges of Antioch and Ma'arra in 1097-98.
- Archaeologists found evidence of cannibalism in a Native American tribe as far back as 1150 in what modern day Colorado is, USA.
- There is evidence that some Tibetan Buddhists consumed pills made from the flesh of deceased people who were believed to have been born as

Brahmins seven times, which could aid in attaining enlightenment.

- Egyptians did it during the severe drought of 1200–1201.
- The French did it; the Waldensians were accused of cannibalism
- Mongols did it as they invaded Vienna, Austria and other European countries to instill fear and just because they liked it. (1240's).
- Marco Polo wrote after he had returned from China that those of a certain region regularly drank the blood and ate the flesh of those they had killed.
- The Italians did it.
- Europeans of the Great Famine of 1315 to 1317 did it. Recall that was how the story of Hansel and Gretel came about from that famine.
- It was done in Sumatra, Indonesia where slave children were purchased from foreign *merchants* for this purpose.

I stop here for a second to say that it is no wonder that God ever repented that He made man because in the heart of man dwells no good thing. In the flesh dwells no good thing. We should be now and eternally grateful for the Lord's great Mercy and patience with us.

- The Aztecs did it.
- The Island Caribs did it.
- Iranians did it in 1503, after defeating their enemies, they ate them.
- In 1514, a captured Hungarian rebel leader was cooked and eaten by his followers. Those who did not comply were also eaten. Those who complied were let go.
- South Americans did it as revenge against their enemies.
- *Mummia* was made and used from the 16th century on. It is called medical cannibalism (In Europe, thousands of Egyptian mummies were ground up and sold as medicine. If this isn't graveyard and witchcraft initiation, I don't know what is.
- The irony is it was thought to stop internal bleeding and to have other healing properties. In a few cases,

*mummia* was still offered in medical catalogues up to the early 20th century.

- Even religious people did this. French Catholics ate the livers and hearts of the Huguenots in the 1572 massacre. Protestants then ate the remains of the Catholic saint, St. Fulcran in a mock eucharist.
- Europeans who had settled in Jamestown Virginia did it from 1609-10 during the period called the starving time. They dug up corpses but one man confessed under torture to having killed, salted, and eaten his pregnant wife;
- The Poles did it. In 1612, Polish troops stationed in Moscow, resorted to cannibalism, in the aftermath of a prolonged siege.
- The Cossacks did it when provisions ran out during an expedition into Siberia, 1643.
- It was done in the Netherlands.

**It was done in the 18th century.**

- Native American tribes of Akokisa and Atakapa of modern-day Texas did it.
- In 1752, Ottawa and Chippewa raided the British Fort Pickawillay where they killed and partially ate at least one English trader and a chief of the Miami people.
- In 1763, Native Americans performed ritual cannibalism on a British soldier during the Siege of Fort Detroit.
- A certain French soldier (1772 – 1798) was a voracious *eater* repeatedly caught consuming corpses stolen from a morgue.
- A Polish soldier was also an insatiable eater, while he served on a French ship in the 1790s.

**19th century**

**1800s and 1810s**

- In New Zealand, 1809 about 66 passengers and crew of

the *Boyd* were killed and eaten by Maori.

- The surviving crew of the ship *Francis Mary* resorted to cannibalism.
- It was done in New Zealand in 1827.

**1830s**

- In New Zealand in the 1830s, a European trader saw that a 15-year-old slave girl was killed with a tomahawk in a Māori village, apparently as punishment for having been absent without permission. She was cannibalized.
- The Portuguese did it to the Africans in the Middle Passage. However, accusations of "White cannibalism" by Black victims of the slave trade were dismissed.

**1840s**

- Canadians did it.
- In the United States, settlers known as the Donner Party resorted to cannibalism while snowbound in the

Sierra Nevada mountains, for the winter of 1846–1847.

- Liver-Eating Johnson reportedly ate the livers of Crow warriors he had slain.

**1850s**

- Boone Helm, AKA, The Kentucky Cannibal, was an American serial killer, who ate human flesh on several occasions between 1850 and 1854 and made no secret of it.
  - Folks, feed the poor and the hungry; in so doing you may save more than the life of that hungry person.
- New Guineans did it in 1858 to Chinese shipwrecked on a French ship.

**1860s**

- In the United States, ten survivors, found nearly two months after a massacre in 1860 on the Oregon Trail had eten five deceased party members.

- 1864, eight Haitians –, four men and four women were convicted to death and executed for having murdered and cannibalized a girl in a Vodou ritual near Port-au-Prince in a money ritual.
- 1866 The Red Lake Chippewa engaged a band of Sioux and celebrated with ritualistic cannibalism afterwards on the international border.

**1870s**

- Alfred Packer, an American prospector was accused of cannibalism during the winter of 1873–1874. sentenced to 40 years in prison.

**1880s**

- 1880–1881 a doomed attempt to explore the route of a Trans-Saharan railway from Algeria to the Sudan-- many members were killed by the Tuaregs. Eventually they resorted to cannibalism on the long retreat through the desert. Only seven survived.

- It was done in Scotland. In 1888, the Scottish whiskey heir, James Jameson says he witnessed and wrote about such.

**1890s**

- Solomon Islands. These are mostly girls and women. Slave girls, especially.
- It was done in Russia, 1892.
- In Congo during the Congo Arab war of 1892–1894. a Belgian commander engaged in cannibalism of the Arab-Swahili soldiers supposedly eating hundreds a day.

**20th century**

**1900s**

- Papua New Guinea, 1901.
- 1902, during the Balundo Revolt
- Tokyo, Japan 1902, an 11-year-old.

**1910s**

- Spain. A seven-year-old.
- An elderly Iraqi couple murdered one adult neighbour and more than a hundred young children in Mosul in 1917.
- The crew members of the US steamship *Dumaru* spent three weeks adrift in a lifeboat, in 1918. Quickly exhausting their supply of food and water, they resorted to cannibalism to survive.
- In Germany, the Butcher of Hanover, sexually assaulted and murdered at least 24 boys, most of them teenagers.

**1920s**

- Cannibalism in Russia, Germany,
- 1926, Catalina, California a man stranded at sea for 11 days had eaten his fishing buddy who may or may not have died of natural causes.
- The American serial killer, Albert Fish murdered at least three children,

afterwards roasting and eating their flesh.

**1930s**

- William Seabrook said he ate human flesh to study its taste.
- Ukraine. Cannibalism was widespread during the famine of 1932. Those who refused to eat corpses died. Those who refused to kill their fellow man died. At least 2,505 people were sentenced for cannibalism in the years 1932 and 1933 in Ukraine, though the actual number of cases was much higher.
- Cannibalism also occurred in the famine in Kazakhstan of 1930–1933. Some consumed corpses, while others committed murders for meat. Villagers "discovered people among them who ate body parts and killed children."
- 1934, a grave robber and suspected serial killer axed to death a couple in Cleveland, Mississippi.

- An Italian woman killed three other women in 1939 and 1940, turning their bodies into teacakes.

**1940s**

- Finland: Finnish soldiers show the skin of Russian soldiers eaten by members of a Soviet patrol during the Continuation War 1942.
- Members of the Leopard Society of Sierra Leon, Liberia, and Cote d'Ivoire, reportedly engaged in cannibalism until the 1940s.
- There are eyewitness accounts of cannibalism during the Siege of Leningrad, (1941–1944),
- Cannibalism, due to a lack of food was practiced in WWII during the Japanese occupation of Hong Kong, (1941–1945).
- 1942 Japanese soldiers' acts of cannibalism among their own troops, on enemy dead, and on Allied prisoners of war.

**1950s**

- In 1950, a Belgian administrator ate a "remarkably delicious" dish in the Belgian Congo made with "the meat ... from a young girl", he found out after eating.
- A few years later, a Danish traveler was served a piece of the "soft and tender" flesh of a slaughtered woman.
- German serial killer, nicknamed the Duisburg Man-Eater practiced cannibalism for 20 years from the mid-1950s, murdering more than a dozen women and girls.
- A tradition of ritualistic cannibalism among the Fore people caused a kuru epidemic, leading to 1000 deaths between 1957 and 1961. Kuru is a disease that people get from eating human flesh.
- Thousands of cases of cannibalism are associated with the Great Chinese Famine of 1959 to 1961.

**1960s**

- In 1961 in Uganda an anthropologist was offered smoked human fingers as well as "a smoked slab of a young woman's buttocks, a truly 'choice cut'" according to the seller.

- 1961, Asmat people allegedly killed and ate Michael Rockefeller in Dutch New Guinea.
- A Czech, in 1963, killed two young boys in a railway wagon to cannibalize them.
- The Wari practiced mortuary cannibalism, until the 1960s.

**1970s**

- 1970, police arrested Stanley Baker on charges of killing and cannibalizing a person from Montana, USA.
- In 1972, Uruguayan Air Force men crashed on a glacier in Argentina. The remaining survivors, including a college rugby team and some of their family members and other passengers, mutually agreed to cannibalism.
- Between 1970 and 1973, a killer raped and murdered between four and

six women in Chicago. The man confessed that he had cut off a piece of flesh from one of the victims' bodies, which he brought back home and ate.

- In 1977 and 1978, the Vampire of Sacramento ate parts of his victims and drank their blood to treat his imaginary illnesses.
- 1979, Albert Fentress lured, killed and cannibalized an 18-year-old high school student.
- 1979 - 1980, in Soviet Kazakhstan, a man killed at least seven women and cannibalized their corpses.

### 1980s

- 8-year-old Tiffany Papesh Maple Heights, Ohio, USA.
- 1981, A Dutch man shot a woman in Paris with cannibalistic intent.
- A Czech, man was a serial killer eater of flesh.
- Rhode Island, USA. a 5-year-old, 1975

- In 1986, Beijing, a married couple killed a teen boy because they wanted to.
- In 1986, American killed and cannibalized a 6-year-old girl.
- In 1988, an artist eats human testicles.
- Man murdered eleven women between 1988 and 1990 in Rochester, NY.
- 1989, New York City resident stabbed woman then boiled and ate her brains then gave out food containing her body parts to the homeless.

**1990s**

- Jeffrey Dahmer, a serial killer Milwaukee, Wisconsin, USA, murdered 17 young men and boys between 1978 and 1991.

When I started this research, Jeffrey Dahmer was the only one that I thought I'd find. This is grievous, how many and how prevalent cannibalism is, but the overview must continue. Dear Reader, I have to make you aware that this is not some isolated thing, it is all too common across what is known as humanity and *civilized* society.

- 1991, Costa Mesa, California, newlywed woman murdered, dismembered, and cannibalized her husband.
- A Soviet Ukraine serial killer was convicted of murdering more than 50 women and children in 1992 and executed two years later.
- A South Korean gang engaged in cannibalism between 1993 and 1994.
- In Brazil, 1995.
- Liberian ex-rebel and warlord Joshua Blahyi confessed in 2008 during the First Liberian Civil War (1989–1997) to various human sacrifices which "included the killing of an innocent child and plucking out the heart, which was divided into pieces to be eaten.
- During that same war crimes trial, chief of operations and head of his alleged "death squad", accused then president, Charles Taylor of ordering his soldiers to commit acts of cannibalism against

enemies, including peacekeepers and United Nations personnel.

- St Petersburg, Russia a man ate three male acquaintances between 1992 and 1997.
- 1999, Indonesia, more than 200 were beheaded and eaten by Dayaks.
- Snowtown murders of South Australia in 1999, two of the murderers fried and ate a part of their final victim in 1999.
- Venezuelan serial killer, killed and ate at least ten men in a period of two years preceding his arrest in 1999.
- 1999, Kazakhstan, three male psychiatric nurses were arrested for killing and eating seven prostitutes.

### 21st century

If you are getting nauseous from reading this, or you have gotten the scope of how demonic and prevalent the eating of human flesh is, skip to the next chapter. It doesn't get any less graphic or potentially triggering in the following section.

### 2000s

- 2000, Australian woman killed her partner, cooked his corpse, to serve it to his children.
- A Chinese performance artist cooked and ate what he claimed to be a human fetus in a staged act entitled "Eating People" in 2000.
- Germany 2001. A young man answered an ad to be slaughtered and eaten, and he was.
- 2001 in Kansas City, Kansas, USA, man goes on a murder spree. Later convicted of murdering four acquaintances, ate one of the victim's legs.
- In July 2002, Ukraine, again.
- In late 2002, Russian brothers.
- 2003, rapper Big Lurch was convicted of the murder and partial consumption of an acquaintance while both were under the influence of PCP.
- In 2003 and 2004, South Korea, a serial killer murdered 21 people, eating the livers of several victims.
- In 2004, 34-year-old killed and cannibalized in East London.

- The Korowai of East Papua still engage in cannibalism.
- Between 2005 and 2006, in India, two men killed at least 19 people, most of them young girls. In a retrial in 2023, the two accused were acquitted of all charges due to a lack of convincing evidence other than their own confessions.
- 2007, French reported that a prison inmate committed cannibalism on a cellmate.
- Turkey, 2007.
- Britain, 2008, British male model arrested for the murder, dismemberment and partial cannibalization of his lover,
- Members of a Satanist youth gang killed four teenagers (three girls and a boy) in Satanic rituals in Russia in 2008.
- 2008, Canada. A 22-year-old Canadian man, stabbed, beheaded on a train, to be eaten.
- 2008, Colombia.
- 2008, five undocumented immigrants from the Dominican Republic OTW to

Puerto Rico ate the flesh of starved companions while lost at sea for 15 days.

- 2009, five members of a tribe in Brazil arrested for murdering and eating a farmer in cannibalism ritual.
- 2009, two men in Russia killed and ate their brother.
- 2012, Japanese authorities convicted three men for killing and eating a man to whom they owed money in 2009.
- 2009, a hysterical woman in San Antonio, Texas, killed her own 3-week-old son and cannibalized parts of the infant's corpse.

**2010s**

- In 2010, PhD student in England, the Crossbow Cannibal, killed and ate three prostitutes.
- Sweden, 2010, man killed and decapitated his girlfriend to eat her flesh.
- Pakistan, 2011, two brothers were arrested for eating a human corpse stolen from a grave. Police also recovered further human remains from their house. They were released but, in 2014, they were making curry out of a human

corpse of a child, presumed to have been stolen from a graveyard.

- 2011, police found body parts of various victims in the refrigerator of serial killer including of two Slovak women who disappeared in 2010.
- 2011, South Korea received a tip that Koreans living in China were smuggling drug capsules into the country with a powder inside made from dead babies.
- 2011, a man killed and ate a homeless man, Bridgeport, Connecticut, USA.
- Brazil, 2012, a man and two women, were arrested for murdering at least two women and eating their flesh.
- 2012, man, 79, accused of killing wife and eating some of her flesh. in Massachusetts, USA. Chinese couple, 6-month immigrants.
- 2012, Miami, Florida, United States, cops shot and killed a man, 31, after he was found naked, eating the face of a homeless man, 65, who survived the attack.

- India, 2012, a couple who owned tea gardens in Assam, India were murdered for cannibalism.
- 2013, Ontario, Canada, a 47-year-old man sexually assaulted and mutilated a 77-year-old woman, eating pieces of flesh he had cut from her body. The victim survived.
- Syria, 2013, a rebel named Abu Sakkar was filmed cutting open the body of a fallen enemy soldier and biting into one of his organs.
- Italy, 2013, a man, 45, discovered by police cooking remains of his 70-year-old mother.
- 2014, a man nicknamed Mad Dog ate the foot of a rival during the Central African African Republic Civil War.
- 2014, a man ate parts of his girlfriend after killing her.
- South Wales, 2014, a man 34, was allegedly found eating the face of a 22-year-old victim in a hotel room.
- 2015, two Mexican cartels were forcing potential recruits to eat the hearts of their victims to jump into the cartel.

- Indonesia, 2015.
- London, 2016 man strangled to death during a sex act. Then the perp cooked and ate parts of the victim.
- Florida, 2016, 19-year-old FSU student...
- 2017, a ring of cannibals arrested by the police and tried in South Africa.
- India 2017, a man killed his mother and ate her heart.
- Russian serial killer arrested in 2018, and found to have killed three people before liquefying and consuming their bodies.
- Michigan, 2019, a 25-year-old male hairstylist hanged by a Grindr date; testicles eaten.

### 2020s

- In 2021, Russia.
- 2021, Fort Worth, Texas.   serial killer killed three and ate the heart of at least one.
- India 2022, three people were arrested for human sacrifice for money ritual.
- 2024, viral video of a Haitian man taking a bite out of a human leg that was on fire.

- 2024, California, A homeless man took the severed leg of a man that was killed by a train chewed on it and was seen hitting walls and other things with it.

*The above information was condensed from and extensive article with ample footnotes:* https://en.wikipedia.org/wiki/Human_cannibalism

The point is that the eating of human flesh by others who *appear* human, as grotesque and unfathomable as it is hasn't stopped from before Christ to even now. Unless we by the power and the Spirit of God stop it! *Drinkers of blood and eaters of flesh,* in the spirit or the natural are most foul. Of course, people want to stop it from happening to them and those whom they love, but what about the rest of the world?

If it is happening in the natural, it started in the spirit realm first. Some of the symptoms of being under attack of *eaters of flesh and drinkers of blood* have been listed. If you suspect or know that is happening to you--, pray. If you do not get relief, seek deliverance.

# Night Pestilence

But thus saith the LORD, Even the captives
of the mighty shall be taken away, and the
prey of the terrible shall be delivered: for I
will contend with him that contendeth
with thee, and I will save thy
children. (Isaiah 49:25)

In Ephesians we read about
principalities, powers, rulers of the darkness
of this world and wicked *spirits* in the
heavenly places. On deliverance ground we
learn that *eaters of flesh and drinkers of
blood* belong to the category of *rulers of the
darkness of this world.* Members of this
group are also territorial demons. In regions
of their rule, they oppress, they depress; they
obsess, they cause mass destruction, and they
afflict. They control the affairs of their
environment. They are wicked. They cause
untimely deaths, accidents, tragedies,
disasters, crises, wars, and violence with the

aim of shedding blood, which serves as their drink, and flesh as their meal.

They attack groups or individuals to suck their blood and eat their flesh. The demise of the victim can be gradual, in which case the victim may just give up.

Knowing that they also eat children in their mother's womb, we must wonder are they the *spirits* that sponsor giving people the idea to have an abortion, working with Molech and or Chemosh to sacrifice the baby. They have been known to eat babies at birth. They are the ones to sponsor bar brawls and murders and homicides, even suicides.

They feed on people's internal organs. Because of this and for other observations I began writing this book. Surgeons have removed gall bladders, appendices, tonsils, all sorts of organs from people for the ages because those organs have become infected, infested, dysfunctional, rebellious, or necrotic and may cause harm to the patient.

This may have become necessary in the natural, after all, Jesus said, If your eye offend you, pluck it out. If an organ is dead or infected, it should be removed, medically speaking.

Again, I ask, *what has* **_spiritually_** *sponsored this?* And will we be asked by God, what happened to your appendix? What about your left lower molar? Where did it go? Did you not have stewardship over it? All body parts have a purpose and a function in the whole and in the health of a person. Shall we disrespect God's order?

All physical illness and sickness has an evil spiritual sponsor. Ask the Lord because it could be *eaters of flesh and drinkers of blood* at work. The danger here is if they are the cause of a lost organ or body structure, then are they in there and planning to take the next part? And the next, and the next until that person is dysfunctional, useless, used up, or unalive completely?

Leprosy was a dread disease in Bible days with no known cure at the time. Today there is a three-antibiotic cure, but back then, before there was a cure, noses fell off, body parts just fell off, until the person eventually succumbed to the disease.

Is this the work of *eaters of flesh &
drinkers of blood*? No doubt.

These demons also operate through
dreams which cause trouble in the physical
realm. There is the manifestation dream—
where what happens in the dream directly
and usually immediately affects the waking
life, and to the negative. Folks, you cannot
remain spiritually dry, you must get prayed
up and stay prayed up.

Today, you have to raise a standard
against them. Stop them before they put a
stop to your existence. They sponsor suicidal
thoughts. Those are not your thoughts; they
are the imaginations and thoughts of demons
and devils!

Demand a stop to their demonic
activities against your life, else they will
terrorize you and torment you and push you
to give up.

12. Every wicked power and *spirit* assigned
    against my health, collide with the Rock
    of Ages today.
13. Destructive infirmities from the powers
    of darkness, assigned to terminate my
    life, die by Fire, in the Name of Jesus.

14. Demonic health arresters, operating in my life, be arrested by Fire, in the Name of Jesus.

15. Every killer disease in my life, I kill you before you kill me, therefore, die, in the Name of Jesus.

16. Every eater of flesh, assigned to eat my flesh, die, in the name of Jesus. *Drinkers of blood,* assigned to drink my blood, fall down and die, in the name of Jesus.

17. My flesh, my blood, reject the voice of death, in the Name of Jesus.

18. Satanic operations in my environment causing massive destruction, backfire, in the Name of Jesus.

*(Some of this chapter and prayer points inspired* by Dr. D.K. Olukoya)

# It Is Done in the Spirit, First

We are talking about spiritual eating of flesh and drinking blood and as usual, if you do nothing about it, it will manifest as disease and bleeding and loss in the natural realm. What we see in the natural has origins in the spiritual realm. This is why the focus on the dream and other spiritual visions are so important.

By coming to Earth, man has chosen and or agreed to move in a very slow realm, that of the flesh. While it may seem that you're having so much fun and time is flying by, you feel that you used to be 25 years old, just a few years ago, but really it's been decades. You may be asking yourself, *Where has the time gone?* The spiritual realm is fast, even instant if you don't take authority where you have authority. The devil is ever busy and, in the spirit, in your dreams you may see a sign or a foretaste of what he has planned. If you do nothing about it, then it is on the way into the flesh realm. Some of those dreams could be trigger dreams or manifestation dreams that are designed to impact the natural realm. In the flesh realm is where it hits, you guessed it, in the flesh.

So, when you see certain signs and symptoms in your dream, you have to deal with them immediately. This may mean you have to deal with things often, like daily. The LORD God is gracious to give you divine dreams. Some of them may not seem divine, but it is God who does two important things for us. First God says that He will not do anything in the Earth unless He first reveals it to His prophets. Thank You, Jesus and Amen.

Secondly, that means that the devil can't do anything to man without first getting permission from God and it can happen when a man is guilty, and not repentant; he becomes lawful prey. Then the devil also has to reveal his plans to that man, especially if that man is in Christ and is prayerful. A lot of man's notifications are in the dream state. Now, whether that man pays any attention to that memo, that notice, that *dream*, vision, or word from another, or not, determines the state of that man, whether he falls or whether he is victorious in any assault that is coming his way. It can determine whether that man lives or dies.

So, in a dream, for instance when a person sees blood, that is not to be looked upon whimsically; it is serious. (Read my book, **When You See Blood**.)

What can be done about it? Dreams, visions, and Words of Knowledge that we get from the Lord must be acted upon. Simply prayed through if they are good prophetic words, or cast down, prayed away if they are demonic plans, plots, and words. We are to cast down evil imaginations. We are to cast down every evil imagination of the devil and his evil agents, and even his evil human agents. That's what the book **Casting Down Imaginations** is about. Therefore, I won't repeat what is in that book, either.

The woman who bleeds and bleeds, in the natural, may have her uterus completely removed if doctors can't stop it with meds, laser ablations or other medical procedures. Some states in the USA are especially known for taking the womb of women with fibroids or repeated fibroids and other womb disorders that cause bleeding. If you live in any of those states, you'd better be prayerful. Might you have to give account to God as to where your uterus went when He sees you in Glory? Might you have to answer if you let the *eaters of flesh* ruin it, destroy it, or take it?

Remember that only about 60 percent, if that, of doctors and nurses, are Christians, some are atheists and others may worship on the dark side, for all we know. So, who will be praying *for* you when you fall ill of anything? Who will be praying for them as they decide your medical fate and health?

Oh, there are no guarantees in the natural. **ONLY GOD** can guarantee how you will be treated by anyone who has the power of life and death over you. If you are not in relationship with God, if you are not prayerful, who will be praying for you? What *spirits*, entities or powers will be influencing the hand of any doctor, nurse or other healthcare person? Oh, they are under Hippocratic Oath? That's nice. That's an oath they state to get that diploma. Who is making them abide by it?

Only God.

We pray they are not in rebellion to God. Of the doctors and nurses who are not Christian or who are not saved, what *god* or *gods* do you think they are serving? You don't know, do you? For example, are they doing a good job because they love people and genuinely want to see people healed? Or, do they only like their job, and they want to continue to make money? Then Mammon is their *god*. Does Mammon care if you are healthy, or not?

You'd better be in close relationship with God, day and night. Pray that you never even need those who do not serve the Lord, but if you do, pray to the Lord.

19. Every blood sucking *spirit*, every flesh eating *spirit*, every familiar *spirit*, ancestral *spirit* monitoring *spirit*, ancient *spirit* looking for blood, catch Fire and burn to ashes, in the Name of Jesus.

20. Catch Fire, catch Fire, catch Fire!

And all these things will be added unto you is the opposite of what witchcraft and satanic powers want to happen to you. Those evil powers want to take from you and take from you, and continue taking from you.

21. *Spirit of death and destruction* and all *eaters of flesh and drinkers of blood*, see the Blood of Jesus and pass over me and my house, in the Name of Jesus.

# Witchcraft

Witchcraft does exist. Witches work for Satan. You cannot fight witchcraft in your flesh or with your mind. Witchcraft unopposed is very powerful. If you were to casually look at anyone, be they a doctor, nurse or any regular person and know the signs of witchy people, such as crystals hanging from their rearview car mirror, lucky items in their possession, dream catchers in their houses, you would either know what they are doing, dealing with, or subject to. They could be a whole witch and not even know it themselves. If you know their dreams, you might know if they've been initiated into the coven and not know it. In this way, by their fruit you would know whom you are dealing with on a daily basis and if you take their counsel or not, whether they be your medical provider or some other businessperson that you pay for consult.

Witches need sacrifices, as said, they work for Satan and Satan is ever looking for sacrifice. They are looking for blood and some are looking for flesh. It is said that spiritual food is cooked up int the covens by witches for the purpose of drinking blood and eating flesh. It is their initiation as well as how they initiate others. They use blood and flesh for their rituals.

Do not be afraid, get prayed up. You can't run. You must deal with what will deal with you as it is dealing with you or before it deals with you.

When you see major diseases, such as heart disease, lung disease, cancer --- there is an evil altar speaking in that family. That altar needs to be torn down.

When you see accidental death and mysterious accidents, incidents, and deaths in a person or groups of people, you can suspect *eaters of flesh and drinkers of blood;* they are looking for a feast. Water deaths may be common. All fires are spiritually suspicious. (Isa 49 24 -30) . These demons sponsor terror attacks as well.

Beelzebub rules over this class of *eaters of flesh and drinkers of blood* demons.

Why are you bleeding? Why are you *still* bleeding? Are you accident prone? Ask yourself all these questions to help spiritual mapping or to discover what *spirits* may be at work against you.

Saints of God, you could be inadvertently ATTRACTING *eaters of flesh and drinkers of blood* to yourself.

*How so?*

You just happen to like certain styles and items so you acquire it and proclaim that it is *style*. Well, it looks witchy. Does God like it?

22. Long nails, witchy nails, pointy nails, curled nails, anything that is or looks like demonic ornamentations on the nails, hair, or body, Lord, make me hate it, in the Name of Jesus.

Tattoos of any kind, but spiders, skulls, dragons, pentagrams and other satanic, demonic and witchy marks and images. It's the style? Whose style? The world's style. So, does God like it?

No. This repulses God. It attracts witches and other entities of the dark kingdom and God has no communion with darkness.

Those dark *spirits* will be attracted to those marks on a person's body, or in a person's house. It is said that demons who recognize these marks as they are flying over will stop when they see "their" mark. Then it is said that they stop to begin to feast on your life because they are *eaters of flesh and drinkers of blood,* and you have identified yourself as one of *theirs*, one who is in league with them. Or, you've shown yourself to be marked as available for them to feast on.

# Hyena & Vulture *Spirits*

Hyenas are fierce little animals that can take down bigger prey than they are.

Vultures eat what is already dead: carrion. You don't want to be food for either of those *spirits*.

23. Every vampire, wolf, werewolf, roaring lion and hyena spirit after my blood, flesh, or life, fall down and die in the Name of Jesus.
24. Let all vultures in any areas of my life be paralyzed, in the Name of Jesus.
25. Let all vultures wishing my spiritual death be paralyzed, in the Name of Jesus.
26. Let every spiritual vulture delegated against me, eat his own flesh, and not mine, and die, in the Name of Jesus.

# Prayers

27. Lord, have Mercy on me, a sinner. I repent and I repent for my parents and ancestors, in the Name of Jesus.
28. Please remove all the iniquity from my bloodline and foundation, in the Name of Jesus.

My flesh and my heart faileth: *but* God *is* th e strength of my heart, and my portion for ever. (Psalm 73:26)

29. Every coven of the witches after my soul, catch Fire and burn to ashes, in the Name of Jesus.
30. Every satanic altar demanding my blood, I command you to be broken into pieces and be consumed by Fire, in the Name of Jesus.
31. Every satanic pot or cauldron cooking any part of my body be utterly destroyed

by the Thunder Hammer of God, in the Name of Jesus.

32. Every body part that is in captivity or has been captured by any coven, jump out, break free, by Thunder and by Fire, in the Name of Jesus.

Blessed be the LORD, who hath not given us as their prey to their teeth. Our sol is escaped as a bird out of the snare of the fowlers: the snare is broken, and we are escaped. (Ps 124 6-7)

33. Any tragedy, death, disaster or loss sent to me, back to sender, in the Name of Jesus.

34. Any covenant of death in my family, any dream of death, any vision of death, I cancel it all by the power in the Blood of Jesus, Amen.

35. Death programmed in dreams, eating in dreams, sex in dreams, injections in dreams, poison in the dream, and any demonic time bomb set to ignite at some certain time, I cancel you by the power in the Blood of Jesus.

36. Every curse of personal destruction or suicide, I break you and the covenant that allowed you, in the Name of Jesus.

37. Every curse of chronic disease or sickness, I break your power over my life, in the Name of Jesus.

38. Every curse of corruption of any organ, I answer you with the stripes of Jesus by which I am healed, in the Name of Jesus.

39. Let all the *eaters of flesh and drinkers of blood* stumble and fall, in the Name of Jesus.

40. Let all *drinkers of blood* and *eaters of flesh* hunting my life stumble and fall, in the Name of Jesus.

41. Any part of my body that is in a pot or a cauldron, jump out by the power that is in the Blood of Jesus.

42. Let all *drinkers of blood* and *eaters of flesh* begin to eat their own flesh and drink their own blood in the Name of Jesus.

43. Cleanse me, Lord. Cleanse me from all evil initiations and from all things occultic, satanic, and or witchcraft related, in the Name of Jesus.

44. Lord, show me things that I am blind to, in the Name of Jesus.

45. Remove every evil mark off of me and every evil marker out of my blood.

46. Let all *eaters of flesh and drinkers of blood* forget my name and become blind to my location, forever, in the Name of Jesus.

47. Cleanse me, cleanse my system, cleanse my foundation, cleanse my bloodline, in the Name of Jesus.

When the wicked, *even* mine
enemies and my foes, came upon me to eat
up my flesh, they stumbled and fell.
(Psalm 27:2)

My knees are weak through
fasting; and my flesh faileth of fatness.
(Psalm 109:24)

48. I will not say in my heart that these nations are greater than I am, but in You, Lord, through you and by Your Spirit, I shall dispossess them, in the Name of Jesus.

Thou shalt say in thine heart, These nations *are* more than I; how can I dispossess them? (Deuteronomy 7:)

49. Lord, give me the mind of Christ and let me keep my wits about me at all times that I don't lose sight of You and Your plans for my life, in the Name of Jesus.

50. Lord, make Your arrows sharp in the hearts of Your enemies, in the hearts of my enemies, in the Name of Jesus.

Thine arrows *are* sharp in the heart of the king's enemies; *whereby* the people fall under thee. (Psalm 45:5)

Therefore did my heart rejoice, and my tongue was glad; moreover also my flesh shall rest in hope: (Acts 2:26)

51. The unfasted man, the carnal man, the idolatrous man...

52. Lord, make Your arrows drunk with the blood of my enemies, in the Name of Jesus.

53. Lord, set the captives free, set me free, in the Name of Jesus.

54. I will make mine arrows drunk with blood, and **my** sword shall devour **flesh**; *and that* with the blood of the slain and of the captives, from the beginning of revenges upon the enemy. (Deuteronomy 32:42)

# Communion

My soul longeth, yea, even fainteth for the
courts of the LORD: my heart and my flesh
crieth out for the living God.  (Psalm 84:2)

In the flesh dwells no good thing, so
when you bring the flesh *under* subjection to
the Spirit of God, then these demons won't
want it. The enemy can't get to you unless
you are defiled. If you keep yourself fasted
and prayed up, they can't touch you. **Make**
your flesh bless the Lord;  if your flesh
blesses the Lord then you have brought it
under and these demons won't want it.

My mouth shall speak the praise of the
LORD: and let all flesh bless his
holy name for ever and ever. (Psalm 145:1)

Dry up the fountains of sin and
iniquity in you, and then the demons won't
want you.

O God, thou *art* my God; early will I
seek thee: my soul thirsteth for
thee, my flesh longeth for thee in a dry and
thirsty land, where no water is; (Psalm 63:1)
The flesh of Christ; if we ask for a
blood transfusion from our own polluted
blood to the Blood of Christ, these demons
can't touch us. If we eat Christ's flesh and
drink His Blood, then we are transformed.
When we put on Christ, we are untouchable.
Then Jesus said unto them, Verily, verily, I
say unto you, Except ye eat the flesh of the
Son of man, and drink his blood, ye have
no life in you.
Whoso eateth my flesh, and drinketh my
blood, hath eternal life; and I will raise him
up at the last day.
For my flesh is meat indeed, and my blood
is drink indeed.
He that eateth my flesh, and drinketh my
blood, dwelleth in me, and I in him.
As the living Father hath sent me, and I live
by the Father: so he that eateth me, even he
shall live by me.
This is that bread which came down from
heaven: not as your fathers did eat manna,
and are dead: he that eateth of this bread
shall live for ever. (John 6:53-58)
We do not take Holy Communion
unworthily so be sure you are saved, repent
of your sins and then take the bread which

has become the Bread of Heaven representing Christ's body which He gave for us. Eat.

Then take the cup which represents the Blood that He shed for us that we may be freed from the Curse of the Law, redeemed from sin, death, hell, and the grave. Redeemed from sickness and poverty into eternal life and in this life, life more abundantly. Redeemed back to the Father and also justified in Christ. Drink.

Be thankful and praise Him!

You have now done what you were supposed to do so that what is not supposed to ever happen to you will not, in the Name of Jesus.

55. I seal these declarations and prayers across every realm, era, age, timeline and dimension, past, present and future, to infinity, with the Blood of Jesus and the Holy Spirit of God.

**56.** All retaliation against these words and prayers backfire against the enemy 1 million fold, to infinity and with Mercy, in the Name of Jesus. **AMEN**

## Dear Reader:

Thank you for acquiring and reading this book. I pray it has set you free. If you don't feel free from praying the prayers once, continue until you get release from the Holy Spirit, or seek a bona fide deliverance minister.

Shalom,

Dr. Marlene Miles

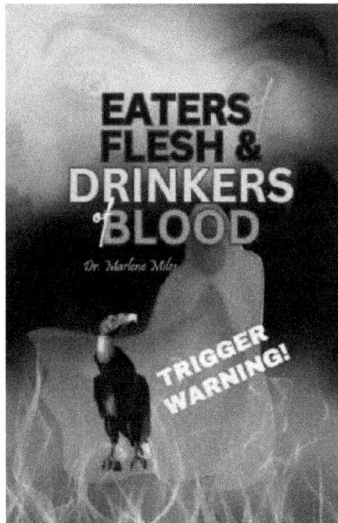

# Prayerbooks by this author

While most books by this author have prayer points either throughout the book or at the end, there are some books that are only prayers. You just open up the book and pray. They are listed below:

**Prayers Against Barrenness:** *For Success in Business and Life*

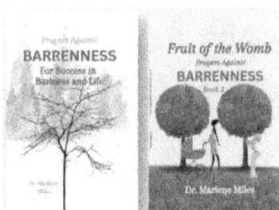

**Fruit of the Womb:** *Prayers Against Barrenness*

**Beauty Curses,** *Warfare Prayers Against*
https://a.co/d/5Xlc20M

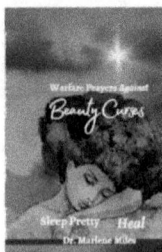

**Courts of Marriage: Prayers for Marriage in the Courts of Heaven** *(prayerbook)*
https://a.co/d/cNAdgAq

## Courtroom Warfare @ Midnight
*(prayerbook)* https://a.co/d/5fc7Qdp

## Demonic Cobwebs *(prayerbook)*
https://a.co/d/fp9Oa2H

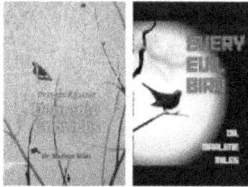

## Every Evil Bird https://a.co/d/hF1kh1O

## Gates of Thanksgiving

## Spirits of Death, Hell & the Grave, Pass Over Me and My House

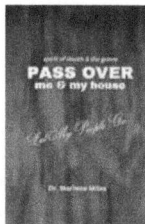

## Throne of Grace: Courtroom Prayer

## Warfare Prayer Against Poverty
https://a.co/d/bZ611Yu

## Other books by this author

AK: The Adventures of the Agape Kid

Already Married in the Spirit: *Why You May Not Be Married in the Natural*

AMONG SOME THIEVES

Ancestral Powers

Anti-Marriage, *The Spirit of*

Backstabbers https://a.co/d/gi8iBxf

Barrenness, *Prayers Against*
https://a.co/d/feUltIs

Battlefield of Marriage, *The*

Beware of the Dog: Prayers Against Dogs in the Dream.

Blindsided: *Has the Old Man Bewitched You?* https://a.co/d/5O2fLLR

Break Free from Collective Captivity

Casting Down Imaginations

Churchzilla, The Wanna-Be, Supposed-to-be Bride of Christ

Curses of Blind Men

Demonic Cobwebs (prayerbook)

Demonic Time Bombs

Demons Hate Questions

Devil Loves Trauma, *The*

Devil Weapons: Unforgiveness, Bitterness,...

The Devourers: Thieves of Darkness 2

Do Not Swear by the Moon

Don't Refuse Me, Lord (4 book series)

https://a.co/d/idP34LG

Dream Defilement

The Emptiers: *Thieves of Darkness, 1*
https://a.co/d/5I4n5mc

Evil Touch

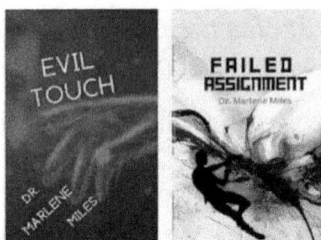

Failed Assignment

Fantasy Spirit Spouse
https://a.co/d/hW7oYbX

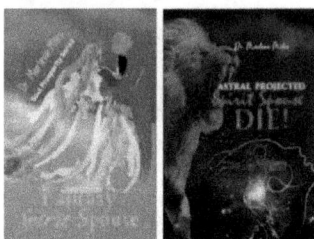

FAT Demons (The): *Breaking Demonic Curses*

The Fold (5-book series)

- The Fold (Book 1)
- Name Your Seed (Book 2)
- The Poor Attitudes of Money (3)
- Do Not Orphan Your Seed (4)
- For the Sake of the Gospel (5)
- My Sowing Journal

Gang Ups: Touch Not God's Anointed

GANG UPS
Touch Not God's Anointed

got HEALING? Verses for Life

got LOVE? Verses for Life

got HOPE? Verses for Life

got money? https://a.co/d/g2av41N

How to Dental Assist

How to Dental Assist2: Be Productive, Not Wasteful

How to STOP Being a Blind Witch or Warlock

I Take It Back

Legacy

Let Me Have A Dollar's Worth
https://a.co/d/h8F8XgE

Level the Playing Field

Living for the NOW of God

Lose My Location
https://a.co/d/crD6mV9

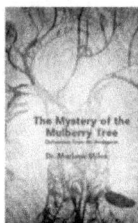

The Robe, Part 1, The Lessons of Joseph

The Robe, Part II, The Lessons of Joseph

Seasons of Grief

Seasons of Waiting

Seasons of War

Second Marriage, Third--, *Any Marriage*

https://a.co/d/6m6GN4N

Sift You Like Wheat

Six Men Short: What Has Happened to all the Men?

Soul Prosperity soul prosperity series 3

https://a.co/d/5p8YvCN

Souls Captivity soul prosperity series 2

The Spirit of Anti-Marriage

The Spirit of Poverty

StarStruck

SUNBLOCK

The Swallowers: *Thieves of Darkness,* 3

Take It Back

This Is NOT That: How to Keep Demons from Coming at You

Time Is of the Essence

Too Many Wives: *Why You Have Lady Problems*

Tormenting Spirits
https://a.co/d/dAogEJf

Toxic Souls

Triangular Power *(series)*

- Powers Above
- SUNBLOCK
- Do Not Swear by the Moon
- STARSTRUCK

Uncontested Doom

Unguarded Hours, *The*

Unseen Life, *The* (forthcoming)

Upgrade: How to Get Out of Survival Mode

- Toxic Souls (Book 2 of series)
- Legacy (Book 3 of series)

The Wasters: *Thieves of Darkness,* Bk 2
https://a.co/d/bUvI9Jo

What Have You to Declare? What Do You Have With You from Where You've Been?

When I Was A Child, *I Prayed As a Child*

# When the Devourer is Rebuked

https://a.co/d/1HVv8oq

**The Wilderness Romance** *(series)* This series is about conducting a Godly relationship and marriage with someone who is a Wilderness person. It is about how to recognize it and navigate through it. These books are about how not to get caught up in such.

- *The Social Wilderness*
- *The Sexual Wilderness*
- *The Spiritual Wilderness*

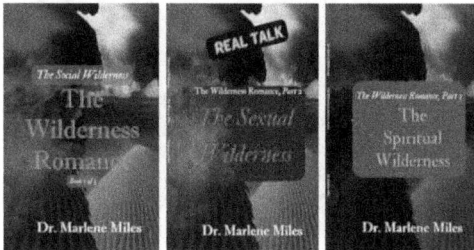

# Other Series

**The Fold (a series on Godly finances)**
https://a.co/d/4hz3unj

**Soul Prosperity Series** https://a.co/d/bz2M42q

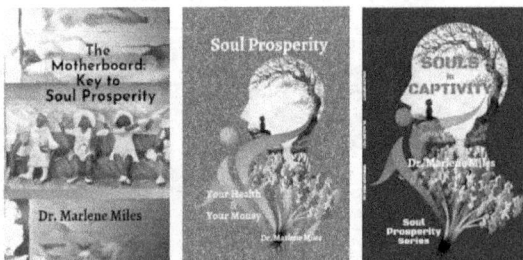

## Spirit Spouse books

https://a.co/d/9VehDSo

https://a.co/d/97sKOwm

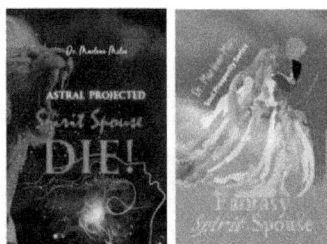

## Thieves of Darkness series

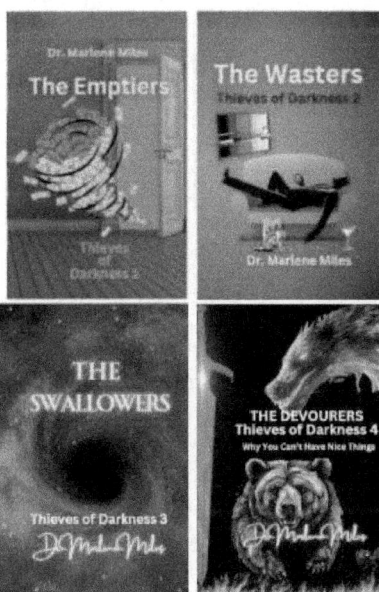

**Triangular Powers** https://a.co/d/aUCjAWC

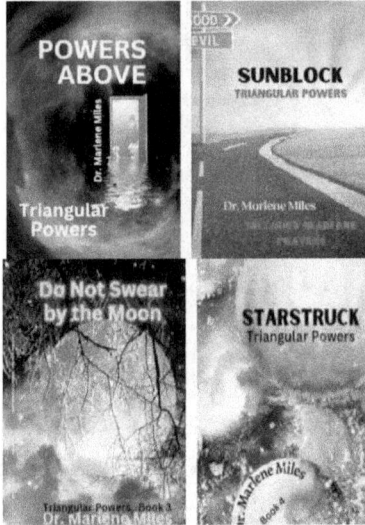

**Upgrade** (series) *How to Get Out of Survival Mode* https://a.co/d/aTERhXO

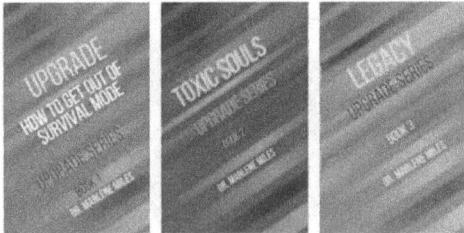

www.ingramcontent.com/pod-product-compliance
Lightning Source LLC
LaVergne TN
LVHW051244080426
835513LV00016B/1738